XO

Love you,
Benny!
Read these works
and see
our faces
& His ♡
♥

# Lift Me Up

# Lift Me Up

CLAIRE DIAZ-ORTIZ

NEW BURLINGTON

A QUARTO BOOK

First published in 2017 by
New Burlington
The Old Brewery
6 Blundell Street
London N7 9BH

ISBN 978-0-85762-608-0

Conceived, designed, and produced by
Quarto Publishing plc
The Old Brewery
6 Blundell Street
London N7 9BH
www.quartoknows.com

QUAR: BQFL

Printed in China

2 4 6 8 10 9 7 5 3 1

# CONTENTS

# WELCOME!

**It is my greatest joy to welcome you here, and to help lift you up on your journey.**

I was lucky to be raised with a Bible by my side. Over the years, the particular look of that big book has changed—a picture book bible for a young me became a tattered teen study guide, which later turned into a leather-bound volume. The message, though, has remained. With every turn of my life, the Bible has given me the wisdom and peace I need to see my way through.

If you were fortunate enough to have a Bible at hand as you grew, you may find many familiar passages in the pages to come. If you are new to God's word, you are about to experience a great gift. I believe with all my heart that the words on these pages can transform.

In my own life, I have seen both deep pain and abiding joy. In all my moments—the good and the bad and all the little ones in between—the Bible has been with me. I believe, with deep conviction, that the Bible can guide you, the Bible can inspire, and the Bible can heal.

The word of God, through the Bible, is the way I know to live this journey.

Life is long, and the Bible will carry us through.

*Chapter One*

# GRATITUDE

I will give thanks
to you, for I am fearfully
and wonderfully made.
YOUR WORKS
ARE WONDERFUL.
My soul knows
that very well.

PSALM 139:14

♥ ♥ ♥ ♥ ♥

Let the word of Christ dwell in you richly; teach and admonish one another in all wisdom; and with GRATITUDE in your hearts sing psalms, hymns, and spiritual songs to God.

COLOSSIANS 3:16

♥ ♥ ♥ ♥ ♥

You are the LIGHT OF THE WORLD. A city located on a hill can't be hidden.

MATTHEW 5:14

# God loves a cheerful giver.

2 CORINTHIANS 9:7

*I am grateful*
TO CHRIST JESUS OUR
LORD, WHO HAS
STRENGTHENED ME,
BECAUSE HE JUDGED ME
*faithful* AND
APPOINTED ME
TO HIS SERVICE,

1 TIMOTHY 1:12

BUT *thanks be to God,* WHO GIVES US THE VICTORY THROUGH *our* LORD JESUS CHRIST.

1 CORINTHIANS 15:57

*O give thanks
to the Lord,
for he is good;
for his steadfast*
**LOVE**
*endures forever.*

1 CHRONICLES 16:34

♥ ♥ ♥ ♥ ♥

# PRAY
# WITHOUT
# CEASING.

1 THESSALONIANS 5:17

♥ ♥ ♥ ♥ ♥

I WILL GIVE YOU THANKS
*with my whole heart*
BEFORE THE GODS,
I WILL SING PRAISES TO YOU.

PSALM 138:1

Give thanks
to him,
BLESS HIS NAME.

PSALM 100:4

# DO NOT WORRY

ABOUT **ANYTHING,**
BUT IN **EVERYTHING**
BY PRAYER AND
SUPPLICATION WITH
*thanksgiving* LET
YOUR REQUESTS BE MADE
KNOWN TO **GOD.**

PHILIPPIANS 4:6

All things were made through HIM.
Without HIM was not anything made that has been made.

JOHN 1:3

YES, EVERYTHING IS FOR YOUR SAKE, *so that grace*, AS IT EXTENDS TO MORE AND MORE PEOPLE, MAY INCREASE THANKSGIVING, TO THE GLORY OF GOD.

2 CORINTHIANS 4:15

You will be enriched in every way for your great generosity, which will produce THANKSGIVING to God through us;

2 CORINTHIANS 9:11

THE HEAVENS DECLARE
the glory of God,
THE EXPANSE SHOWS HIS
handiwork.

PSALM 19:1

Jesus Christ is the same yesterday, today, and forever.

HEBREWS 13:8

They will mount up
with wings like EAGLES.
They will run, and not be
weary. They will walk,
and not faint.

ISAIAH 40:31

# You are the God who does WONDERS.

PSALM 77:14

# *Prayer prompts on the theme of*

# GRATITUDE

1. *When you wake in the morning*, give a quick thanks to God for another bright day. (Even before you lift your head from the pillow and put your feet on the floor!)

2. *In your morning bath or shower*, take a moment to be grateful for hot water, clean soap, and a new you each and every day.

3. *Are you standing* before your closet not sure what you want to wear today? Thank God for the opportunity to choose.

4. *Taking your first sip of water* for the day, thank God for the chance to wash your soul clean each morning.

5. *Before your first meal of the day*—and every meal thereafter—take a brief breath to thank God for the blessing of having food in front of you.

6. *Bitterly cold outside?* Too hot to bear? Give gratitude to God for spinning seasons that never cease to turn Winter into Spring.

7. *Did you see someone today who made you smile?* Thank God for putting him or her in your life to brighten your days.

8. *Does someone around you today need a listening ear*, or a friendly hug? Thank God for placing you in their path to help them get through the day.

9. *Tired in the middle of a long afternoon?* Thank God that tonight a soft bed awaits.

10. *Having a cup of tea*, coffee, or chocolate? Thank God for making it so good.

11. *Did you have a moment today* that filled you to the brim with happiness and joy? Thank God that these moments exist, and ask Him to help you find them—more easily and more often— in even the smallest of places.

12. *Did something hard happen to you today?* Something that pierced your soul ever so slightly (or far too much)? Thank God for being there in the midst of the trials.

**13.** *Did you catch the sunset?* Or happen upon a star in a dark sky? Thank God for bringing another day to its close.

**14.** *As you get in bed to fall asleep,* thank God for three things that happened today. No matter how big, or how small, find three small things. Every day.

**15.** *The power to thank others* is one of the greatest tools that God bestowed on us. Use it well, and use it often.

**16.** *Gratitude flourishes* when we remember the small things. Today, remember the smallest of those things, and your gratitude will expand.

**17.** *Thank God to thank God.* Sound confusing? It is by thanking God that our thanks for God grows.

**18.** *Planting the seeds of gratitude* is an essential practice to letting thanks live louder in your life. Today, plant the small seeds of thankfulness that you see around you.

**19.** *Gratitude is breath.* With each and every breath you take, thanks be to the God above.

**20.** *Gratitude is a practice.* Practice yours today by remembering to give thanks for three things you see when the clock strikes three.

**21.** *Sometimes, we can give thanks* to someone without saying a word. Today, thank someone with your smile.

**22.** *Thankfulness and gratitude* go hand in hand to build a better life. Today, give thanks for the chance to be grateful in all you do.

**23.** *The way to banish comparison?* Gratitude. Whenever you enter into thoughts that encourage you to compare and despair, build yourself up with God's gratitude all over again.

**24.** *There is a power in gratitude* that cannot be underestimated. The moment you give thanks, that is the moment you feel your heart expand.

**25.** *A life well lived* depends on a life well thanked. Give thanks for yours, today.

**26.** *True gratitude is the sweetest peace* you can ever know.

**27.** *Open your heart to gratitude,* and see how your life expands.

**28.** *Quick to anger?* Give thanks for the world at your feet before you share a harsh word.

**29.** *Quick to complain?* Give thanks for your blessings before you cry about your lack.

**30.** *Quick to whine?* Give thanks for all you have before you let loose with all you are missing.

**31.** *Finally, in all you do,* thank God for the chance to learn to be ever more grateful for this one, sweet life.

Chapter Two

# WORRY

He ANSWERED me, and DELIVERED me from all my FEARS.

PSALM 34.4

You are of God, LITTLE CHILDREN,
AND HAVE OVERCOME THEM;
BECAUSE GREATER IS HE
WHO IS IN YOU
THAN HE WHO IS IN THE WORLD.

1 JOHN 4:4

THEREFORE *don't be anxious*, SAYING, 'WHAT WILL WE EAT?', 'WHAT WILL WE DRINK?' *or*, 'WITH WHAT WILL WE BE CLOTHED?'

MATTHEW 6:31

Who of you by worrying can add a single hour to your life?

LUKE 12:25

# SEE THE BIRDS OF THE SKY, **THAT THEY DON'T SOW**, NEITHER DO THEY REAP, NOR GATHER INTO BARNS. YOUR HEAVENLY FATHER FEEDS THEM. AREN'T YOU OF MUCH *more* VALUE THAN THEY?

MATTHEW 6:26

# THERE IS NO FEAR IN LOVE, BUT PERFECT LOVE CASTS OUT FEAR;

1 JOHN 4:18

BUT *seek* FIRST GOD'S KINGDOM, AND HIS RIGHTEOUSNESS; AND ALL THESE THINGS WILL BE GIVEN TO YOU AS WELL.

MATTHEW 6:33

THEREFORE
**DON'T BE ANXIOUS**
FOR TOMORROW,
FOR TOMORROW WILL
BE ANXIOUS FOR ITSELF.

MATTHEW 6:34

**DON'T** let your heart be troubled, **NEITHER** let it be fearful.

JOHN 14:27

Charm is deceitful, and
BEAUTY IS VAIN,
but a woman who fears
the LORD is to be praised.

PROVERBS 31:30

Worry
·········

WHOEVER **FEARS** THE **LORD** HAS A *secure fortress,* AND FOR THEIR CHILDREN IT WILL BE A **REFUGE.**

PROVERBS 14:26

# IN THE SAME WAY, THE **SPIRIT** ALSO HELPS OUR WEAKNESSES.

ROMANS 8:26

FOR HE SAYS,
"At an acceptable time
I listened to you,
in a day of
salvation
I helped you."

2 CORINTHIANS 6:2

# BUT SHE CAME AND WORSHIPPED HIM, SAYING, *"Lord, help me."*

MATTHEW 15:25

For in that he himself has **SUFFERED** being tempted, he is able to help those who are tempted.

HEBREWS 2:18

LET US THEREFORE DRAW NEAR WITH BOLDNESS TO THE **THRONE OF GRACE**, THAT WE MAY RECEIVE MERCY, AND MAY FIND GRACE FOR HELP IN **TIME OF NEED**.

HEBREWS 4:16

# GOD IS NOT UNJUST;
HE WILL NOT FORGET YOUR
**WORK** AND THE **LOVE** YOU HAVE
SHOWN HIM AS YOU HAVE
HELPED HIS PEOPLE AND
CONTINUE TO HELP THEM.

HEBREWS 6:10

SO THAT WITH GOOD
COURAGE WE SAY,
*"The Lord is my helper.
I will not fear.
What can man do
to me?"*

HEBREWS 13:6

HE REPLIED, "**BECAUSE YOU HAVE SO LITTLE FAITH**. TRULY I TELL YOU, IF YOU HAVE FAITH AS SMALL AS A MUSTARD SEED, YOU CAN SAY TO THIS MOUNTAIN, *'Move from here to there,'* AND IT WILL MOVE.

MATTHEW 17:20

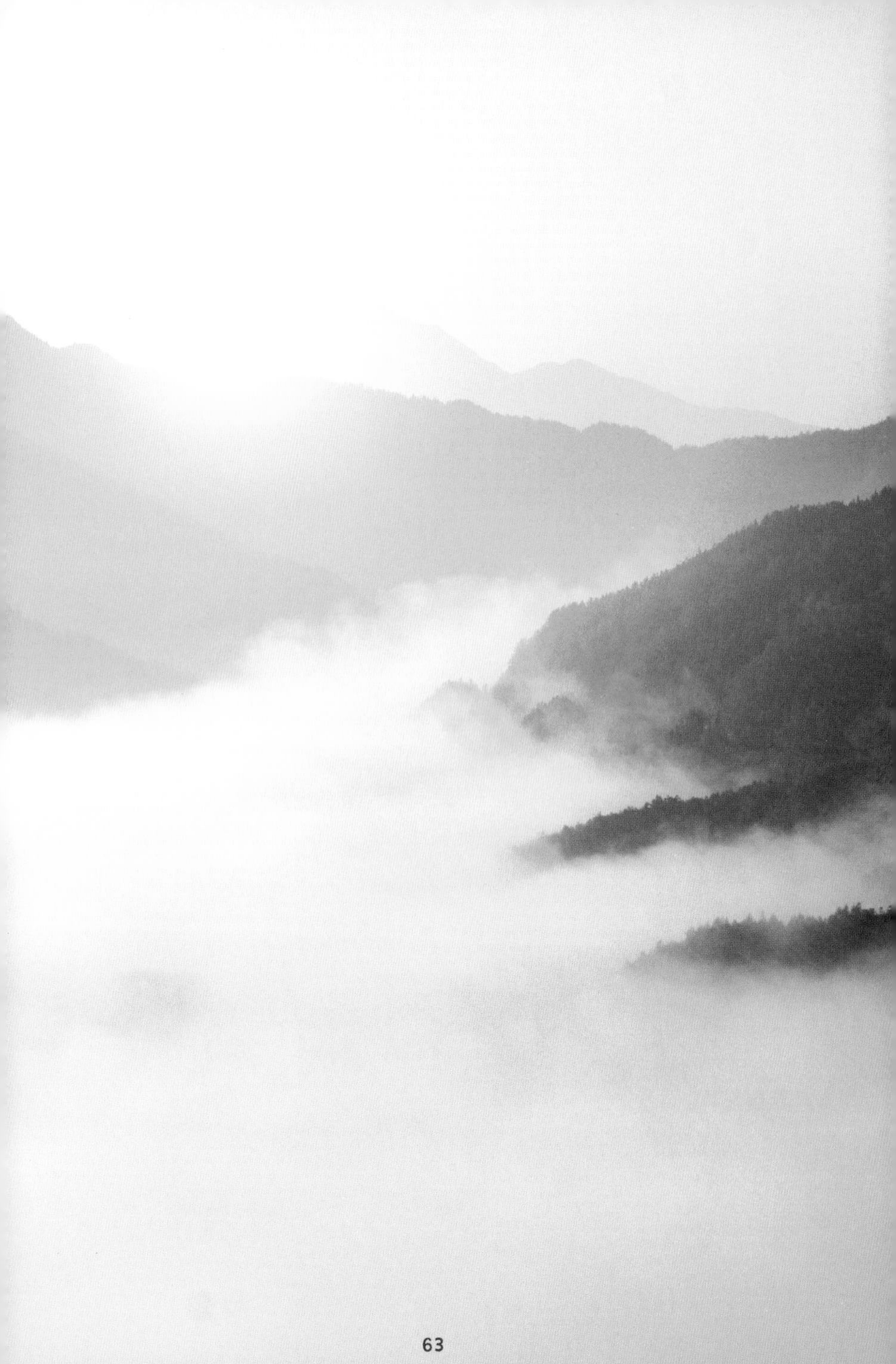

# Prayer prompts on the theme of

## WORRY

1. **Does worry start the moment you wake in the morning?** Breathe into God's love to start your day.

2. **Don't let worry take over your dreams.** Always take a moment to pray before laying down your head.

3. **Worry tends to overwhelm** a life otherwise full of love. Whenever you feel worry raising its ugly head, ask God to help you see the good in the world around you.

4. **Worry tries to trick us** into believing that all is lost. Nothing could be further from the truth. Banish worry, and find your peace.

5. **Sometimes, worry starts as something small,** but the attention we give it makes it grow. Ask God to help you to see worry for the small thing it is today, and not the big thing you have made it become.

6. **With God by your side,** no worry is too great for this life.

7. **Worry keeps us all from living our best lives.** Today, banish worry with gratitude.

8. **Worry divides.** Today, if you see worry on the face of another, offer them a listening ear.

9. **Lift up those you see** in the midst of their worry. Show them the road to God's peace.

10. **One good prayer?** Help, God, help. Share your worries with God today, and feel greater peace tomorrow.

11. **We all have particular moments** in the day when worry most often strikes. Early morning, say, or late at night. Whenever it is, you are at your most pressed, ask God to guard your heart.

12. **As humans, we know how to worry.** As children of God, we are called to let God do the worrying for us.

**13.** *In the midst of your deepest worries*, ask God to show you a moment of calm. Then, ask God to extend that moment.

**14.** *Worry and gratitude cannot exist together*. Banish worry with gratitude to God.

**15.** *Worry comes to all of us*, and with it comes God. Invite God to help you in your worries, and your worries will lessen.

**16.** *All our lives are touched by worry*, and all our lives are embraced by God. Let God be greater than your worry.

**17.** *Sometimes, even in the midst of a wonderful moment*, a worry can enter in. In that moment—and especially in those moments—ask God to shine His light on the good.

**18.** *There is no way to be without worry in a broken world*. There is only God, and God is enough.

**19.** *Being mindful that worry is a natural part of a broken world* can help us to not be surprised when it enters, once again. With God, you can overcome it.

**20.** *A good God* is no match for worry.

*Chapter Three*

## SORROW

for we WALK
BY FAITH
not by sight.

2 CORINTHIANS 5:7

WHEN YOU PASS
THROUGH THE
*waters,*
*I will be*
WITH *you;*

ISAIAH 43:2

♥ ♥ ♥ ♥ ♥

# I WILL CALL TO YOU WHEN MY *heart* IS OVERWHELMED. LEAD ME TO *the Rock* THAT IS HIGHER THAN I.

PSALM 61:2

♥ ♥ ♥ ♥ ♥

*God promises* TO MAKE SOMETHING *good* OUT OF THE STORMS THAT BRING DEVASTATION TO YOUR LIFE.

ROMANS 8:28

# "A LITTLE WHILE, AND *you will not see me.* again A LITTLE WHILE, *and you will see me.*"

JOHN 16:16

SORROW IS *better than laughter;* FOR BY THE SADNESS OF THE FACE THE HEART IS MADE **GOOD**.

ECCLESIASTES 7:3

THEREFORE *shake off your great sadness* AND LAY ASIDE YOUR MANY SORROWS, SO THAT THE MIGHTY ONE MAY BE MERCIFUL TO YOU AGAIN.

2 ESDRAS 10:24

and sorrow and sighing will flee away.

ISAIAH 35:10

He will wipe every tear from their eyes. Death will be no more;

**REVELATION 21:4**

BUT NOW *trouble* *comes to you*, AND YOU ARE DISCOURAGED; IT STRIKES YOU, AND YOU ARE DISMAYED.

JOB 4:5

# MY EYES HAVE GROWN DIM WITH GRIEF; MY WHOLE FRAME IS *but a shadow.*

JOB 17:7

# DON'T LET YOUR HEART BE TROUBLED.
## Believe in God.
# BELIEVE ALSO IN ME.

JOHN 14:1

# FOR HE DOES NOT WILLINGLY AFFLICT or GRIEVE ANYONE.

LAMENTATIONS 3:33

I behaved MYSELF as THOUGH IT HAD BEEN MY FRIEND OR MY BROTHER. I bowed down mourning, AS ONE WHO mourns HIS MOTHER.

PSALM 35:14

MY EYE GROWS DIM THROIGH SORROW. EVERY DAY I CALL ON YOU, O LORD; I spread out my hands to you.

PSALM 88:9

# FOR THOUGH HE CAUSE GRIEF, *yet he will have compassion* ACCORDING TO THE MULTITUDE OF HIS LOVING KINDNESSES.

LAMENTATIONS 3:32

# *Prayer prompts on the theme of*

## SORROW

1. **The feeling of sorrow is real.** Don't push it down or shove it away. Feel it, and feel God work in you to help you heal.

2. **Sorrow comes and goes** throughout the course of a day. With prayer, let it ebb and flow as it needs to.

3. **In the dark of night, sorrow** can be at its worst. Find yourself awake in the middle of the night? Ask God to heal your sorrows.

4. **Grief is necessary to heal.** It's hard to embrace sorrow, but ask God to show you how.

5. **Times of sorrow don't stay forever.** If you are in the midst of sorrow, find small ways to remember through God that this is one season of many to come.

6. **Sorrow doesn't just come and go** in the course of a day—sorrow also ebbs and flows with the changing seasons. Today's sorrow can turn to tomorrow's joy.

7. **Sadness enters all of our lives.** If we invite God in, He can enter, too.

8. **Feel the sorrow, and live anyway.** God will guide you.

9. **When we are in the midst of our deepest sorrow,** it can be hard to remember that a loving God is eager to guide us to joy. Open your heart to God to get closer to God's joy.

10. **Sorrow can come at all stages of our lives.** At each stage, God wants to walk with us. Let Him do so.

11. **In the very darkest of moments,** it can sometimes be hard to remember that God is there. Even when you feel at your worst, remember that you are not alone.

12. **If you are in the midst of deep sorrow,** waking anew each day to that same sorrow can be hard. Start your days with God and ask Him to walk with you.

**13.** *God wants to meet us* in our sorrow. Open the door to let Him heal you.

**14.** *The simplest of prayers can sometimes be the best.* Tell God how sad you are, and watch Him lift you up.

**15.** *Sorrow comes with pain.* God knows that pain more than anyone else. Pray to Him to be with you in your hurt.

**16.** *Sometimes sorrow comes* from disappointment. If you are disappointed by a big or little thing in your life, ask God to be with you in your sorrow.

**17.** *When you hurt, God hurts.* When you hurt, God wants to help. Pray to God to help you in your hurt.

**18.** *When we cry out to God,* God hears us. Let Him hear your cries.

**19.** *Never be ashamed* to weep in front of God. Your father wants to hear your every sadness, and wants to be with to help you heal. Pray to Him.

**20.** *Let sorrow be a small* moment in a long life. With God, it can be.

# Chapter Four

## LOVE

# Be kind.

EPHESIANS 4:32

♥ ♥ ♥ ♥ ♥

# KEEP YOUR **HEART** WITH ALL DILIGENCE, FOR OUT OF IT IS THE
## *wellspring of life.*

PROVERBS 4:23

♥ ♥ ♥ ♥ ♥

FOR THE MOUNTAINS MAY DEPART, AND THE HILLS BE REMOVED; BUT MY *loving kindness* WILL NOT DEPART FROM YOU,

ISAIAH 54:10

Greet one another with a KISS OF LOVE.
Peace be to you all who are in Christ Jesus.
AMEN.

1 PETER 5:14

IF I SPEAK WITH THE **LANGUAGES OF MEN AND OF ANGELS,**
BUT DON'T HAVE LOVE,
*I have become sounding brass,*
OR A CLANGING CYMBAL.

1 CORINTHIANS 13:1

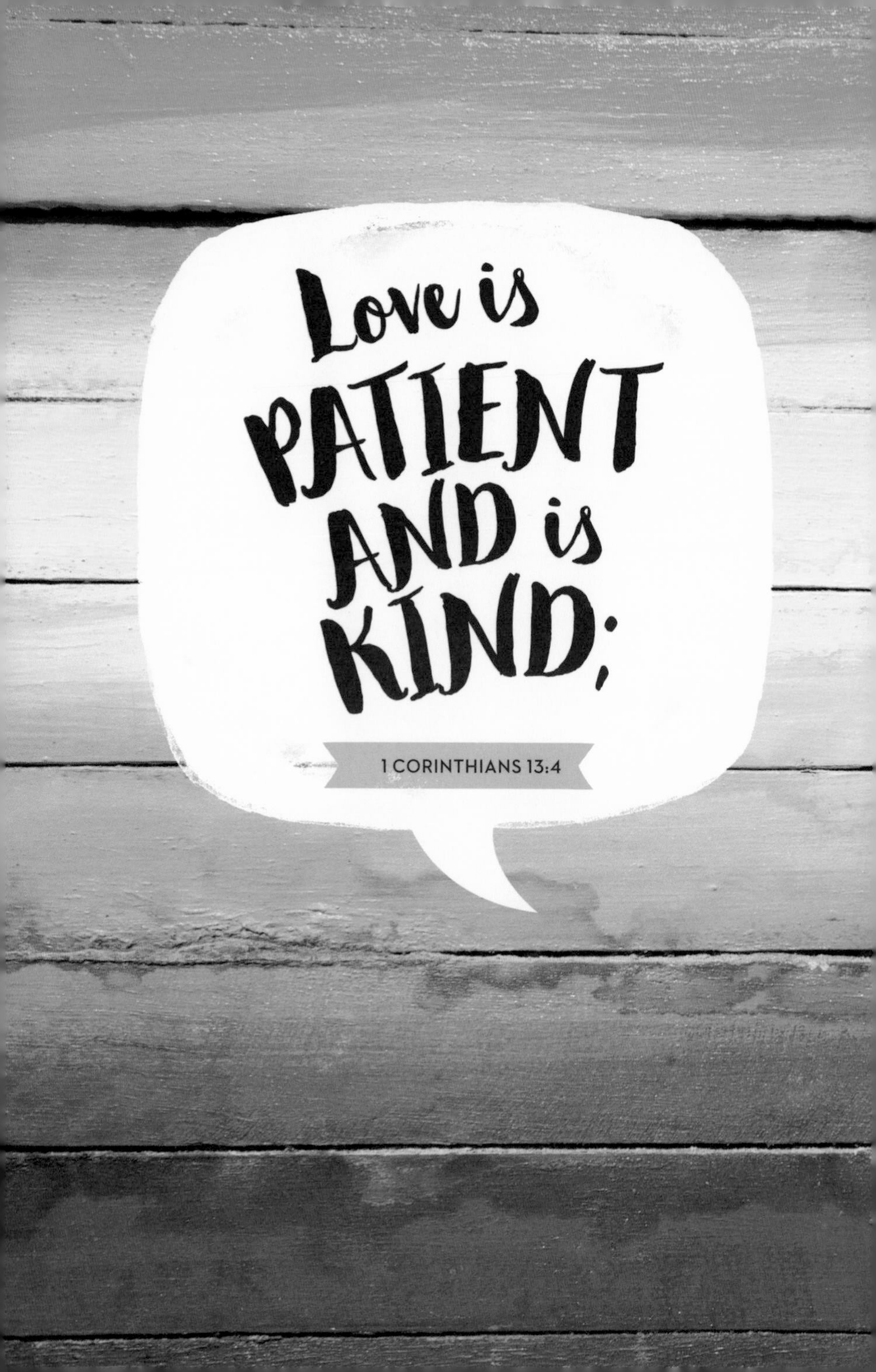
Love is
PATIENT
AND is
KIND;
1 CORINTHIANS 13:4

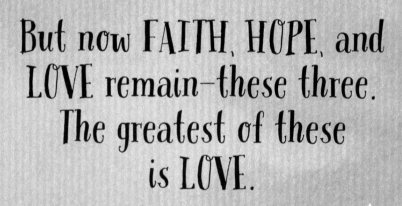

But now FAITH, HOPE, and LOVE remain—these three. The greatest of these is LOVE.

1 CORINTHIANS 13:13

Love

JESUS SAID TO HIM,
*"You shall love the Lord your God*
WITH ALL YOUR HEART, WITH
ALL YOUR SOUL, AND WITH ALL
YOUR MIND."

MATTHEW 22:37

LOVE NEVER FAILS.

1 CORINTHIANS 13:8

IF YOU **LOVE** THOSE WHO **LOVE** YOU, WHAT CREDIT IS THAT TO YOU? FOR EVEN SINNERS LOVE THOSE *who love them.*

LUKE 6:32

FOR GOD *didn't* GIVE US A SPIRIT OF FEAR, BUT OF *power, love,* AND *self-control.*

2 TIMOTHY 1:7

# SPEAK OUT
## *for those*
# WHO CANNOT SPEAK.

PROVERBS 31:8

BUT I SAY TO YOU, LOVE YOUR ENEMIES AND **PRAY** FOR THOSE WHO PERSECUTE YOU,

MATTHEW 5:44

FOR *God so loved* THE WORLD, THAT HE **GAVE HIS ONE AND ONLY SON,** THAT WHOEVER BELIEVES IN HIM SHOULD NOT PERISH, BUT HAVE ETERNAL LIFE.

JOHN 3:16

# The FATHER loves the SON, and has given all things into his hand.

JOHN 3:35

Therefore the
FATHER LOVES ME,
because I lay down
my life, that I may
take it again.

JOHN 10:17

I GIVE YOU A **NEW**
**COMMANDMENT**, THAT YOU
*love one another.* JUST AS I
HAVE LOVED YOU,
YOU ALSO SHOULD
LOVE ONE ANOTHER.

JOHN 13:34

# EVEN AS THE FATHER HAS *loved me*, I ALSO HAVE LOVED YOU. REMAIN IN MY LOVE.

JOHN 15:9

# NO ONE HAS *greater love* THAN THIS, TO LAY DOWN ONE'S LIFE FOR ONE'S FRIENDS.

JOHN 15:13

# YOU SHALL **SEEK ME**, AND **FIND ME**, WHEN YOU SHALL SEARCH FOR ME *with all your heart.*

JEREMIAH 29:13

Who shall separate us
from the love of Christ?
Could oppression, or
anguish, or persecution,
or famine, or nakedness,
or peril, or sword?

ROMANS 8:35

**NO**, IN ALL THESE THINGS,
WE ARE MORE THAN
CONQUERORS THROUGH
HIM WHO LOVED US.

ROMANS 8:37

# LET LOVE BE GENUINE;
## hate what is evil,
## hold fast to what is good;

ROMANS 12:9

# I AM WITH YOU
## always,

MATTHEW 28:20

But **LOVE YOUR ENEMIES,**
and do good, and lend,
expecting nothing back; and
your reward will be great,

LUKE 6:35

For your great LOVING kindness reaches to the heavens, and your TRUTH to the skies.

PSALM 57:10

# FOR THE WHOLE LAW IS FULFILLED IN ONE WORD, IN THIS: **"YOU SHALL LOVE YOUR NEIGHBOR AS YOURSELF."**

GALATIANS 5:14

# THERE IS no FEAR IN LOVE;

1 JOHN 4:18

# Prayer prompts on the theme of

## LOVE

1. *Wake in the morning* and see the light of the day. This is the light is love.

2. *Every day, thank God* for another day on this bright earth—another day to show your love.

3. *Remember that loving others* is one of the best things you can do for your soul.

4. *Think of one person* you can love today. Then, go out and love them.

5. *Send a note of love* to one person you care for.

6. *Send a message of love* to one acquaintance you don't know well. Don't startle them with your emotion—just take a moment to send well wishes.

7. *Love is kindness.* Be kind to someone you don't know today.

8. *Sometimes we say,* "I love you," without thinking about the meaning behind those words. Today, say "I love you" not as a reflex, but as a statement of truth.

9. *Love is patient.* Today, be patient in one thing—show your love.

10. *Love never boasts.* How can you be humble today to better show your love?

11. *Love is steady.*

12. *The daily work of love* is not fancy. Instead, it can look like the washing of dishes and the cleaning-up of a messy room. What small thing did you today that was really an act of love?

13. *Love shows up.* Does someone in your life need extra love today? Pray to know who it is, and then show them love. Show up.

14. *God loves us* more than we can ever hope to love another. Accept God's love.

15. *It is God's love for us* that teaches us how to love. After all, who is best to model love than the one who loves us above all else? What can you do today to model God's love for you with the world?

**16.** *Love is service.* How can you serve another person today to show your love?

**17.** *Gifts can show love.* Is there a gift you can give someone today that will show them how much you care? Think small and inexpensive, and you'll find a true path to loving them.

**18.** *Love is time with another.* How can you spend time with someone you love today as a way to show your love for them?

**19.** *Love is time with God.* Show your love for God by spending time with Him today.

**20.** *Love doesn't always have the right words.* Have you ever wanted to show love, but worried you don't have the right words? Love is there, no matter what words come out.

**21.** *Affection is love.* Can you show affection for someone today as a way to show your love for them?

**22.** *Love is the antidote to fear.* When in fear, spread God's love.

**23.** *God has given us all the gift* of love. Use your gift today to share His love with the world.

**24.** *Love is gratitude.* Thank God today for the love you have in the world.

**25.** *There are times* when the last thing we want to do is extend love to another. In those times—and mostly in those times—it is up to you to push through to love.

**26.** *In anger, we lose our way* to love. Ask God to help you find the journey back.

**27.** *Every day, in every way,* love beats out fear. Do you fear? Then ask God for love.

**28.** *Love for God is the greatest love* there is. Tell God of your love for Him in your prayers.

**29.** *Every day, we have a new chance* to show our love. Show yours, today. Then, show yours, tomorrow.

Chapter five

# PEACE

*Blessed* ARE THE
PEACEMAKERS, FOR
THEY SHALL BE CALLED
**CHILDREN OF GOD**.

MATTHEW 5:9

# INTO WHATEVER HOUSE *you* ENTER, FIRST SAY, *"Peace be to this house."*

LUKE 10:5

Jesus therefore said to them again, "Peace be to you. As the FATHER has sent me, even so I SEND YOU."

JOHN 20:21

# PEACE I LEAVE WITH you.

JOHN 14:27

NOW MAY THE GOD OF
HOPE FILL YOU WITH ALL
**JOY AND PEACE** IN BELIEVING,
THAT YOU MAY ABOUND
IN HOPE, IN THE POWER
OF THE *Holy Spirit.*

ROMANS 15:13

If it is possible,
AS MUCH AS IT IS UP TO YOU,
be at peace
WITH ALL MEN.

ROMANS 12:18

HE CAME AND PREACHED *peace to you* WHO WERE FAR OFF AND TO THOSE WHO WERE NEAR.

EPHESIANS 2:17

# AS **SHOES** FOR YOUR **FEET** PUT ON WHATEVER WILL MAKE YOU READY TO PROCLAIM THE **GOSPEL OF PEACE.**

EPHESIANS 6:15

And the peace of GOD, which surpasses all understanding, will guard your hearts and your thoughts in CHRIST JESUS.

PHILIPPIANS 4:7

THE THINGS WHICH YOU *learned, received, heard, and saw in me:* DO THESE THINGS, AND THE **GOD OF PEACE** WILL BE WITH YOU.

PHILIPPIANS 4:9

MAY THE **GOD** OF
**PEACE** HIMSELF
SANCTIFY
YOU COMPLETELY.

1 THESSALONIANS 5:23

For he is
our peace.

EPHESIANS 2:14

Pursue PEACE with everyone,
and the holiness without which
no one will see the LORD.

HEBREWS 12:14

Now the fruit of righteousness is sown in peace by those who make peace.

JAMES 3:18

TAKE *delight* IN
THE LORD AND HE
WILL GIVE YOU
THE DESIRES OF
YOUR *heart.*

PSALM 37:4

# MERCY to you and PEACE and LOVE be multiplied.

JUDE 1:2

BUT THE **WISDOM** THAT IS FROM
ABOVE IS FIRST PURE, THEN
**PEACEFUL, GENTLE,**
REASONABLE, FULL OF MERCY
AND GOOD FRUITS, WITHOUT
PARTIALITY, AND
WITHOUT HYPOCRISY.

JAMES 3:17

**GRACE** TO YOU AND **PEACE**
BE MULTIPLIED IN THE
KNOWLEDGE OF GOD AND OF
JESUS OUR LORD.

2 PETER 1:2

# Prayer prompts on the theme of

## PEACE

**1.** *There is peace in stillness.* Be still, and find your peace.

**2.** *Ask for the peace* you need when you need it most from God.

**3.** *An early moment of peace* is one of the smartest things you can do for your day. When you wake, try to find peace in a small moment, and then let that peace carry you throughout the rest of your hours.

**4.** *Sometimes, in the midst of the busy,* we forget that peace exists all around us if we just reach out. Reach out, now.

**5.** *Trying to find peace* when you are far from it is hard, but it is possible. Ask God to guide you back.

**6.** *Praying for peace* is one of the best prayers you can make each and every day. Try it today, now. Peace, God, please.

**7.** *Sending peace* to those you know and don't is one wonderful way to feel more connected with those around you. Offer them peace through your prayers, whether they know it or not.

**8.** *There is a still, small peace inside you.* Ask God to help reveal it to you today.

**9.** *Some of the darkest times* of our lives hide beneath them the deepest peace we can ever know. Pray to God to reveal where His peace is hidden in your circumstances.

**10.** *Peace is everywhere,* but peace can feel elusive. Ask God to make it clear where peace lies in your life.

**11.** *Some days it feels that life is out of control,* and that you are at the mercy of its whims. Remembering the peace within you, given to you by God, is the only way to find your way home on these days.

**12.** *God lives in the peaceful moments.* When you feel yourself far from God, cultivate a moment of peace to bring you home to Him.

**13**. *The Prince of Peace* has a deep desire for your life, and it is a desire for pure peace. Ask God to help you find it.

**14.** *Remember this.* Peace is your North star. Peace can guide you home.

**15.** *There is a wonderful world* of peace just beneath the surface of our busy days. Ask God to reveal His peace to you.

**16.** *God is all around us every day.* But God loves to live in peace. When you are far from peace, call God to you. God will come, and so will peace.

**17.** *There are moments of peace* under the surface. God has offered to help us unearth them. We just have to ask.

**18.** *Peace is a place made by God.* It is a place we can return to, day in and day out. Find the place of peace, and return, always.

**19.** *At all stages of life*, peace can be hard to be find but wonderful to revel in. Revel in the peace of God when you find it.

**20.** *The deepest peace* is the peace of knowing that God's peace is infinite.

# INDEX

# CREDITS

## KEY

Chapter and verse
references according to
source as follows

■ = **NRSV** (New Revised
Standard Version Bible)

■ = **NIV** (New International
Version)

■ = **WEB** (The World
English Bible)

AlinaMD/Shutterstock.com, p28
amenic181/Shutterstock.com, p50
ANADMAN BVBA/Shutterstock.com,
p126
Anastasia Tveretinova/Shutterstock.com,
p42
AnaWhite/Shutterstock.com, p33
Ann Doronina/Shutterstock.com, p118, 44
Antonio Guillem/Shutterstock.com,
p140-141
Artith chotitayangkoon/Shutterstock.com,
p73
astarot/Shutterstock.com, p116-117
Atomazul/Shutterstock.com, p60
azyllama/Shutterstock.com, p98-99
bbearlyam/Shutterstock.com, p30-31
Bogdan Sonjachnyj/Shutterstock.com, p10
Brett Allen/Shutterstock.com, p79
Brocreative/Shutterstock.com, p77
Calesh/Shutterstock.com, p1, 32, 49, 52,
64-65, 86, 100, 128-129
CHOATphotographer/Shutterstock.com,
p143
DGLimages/Shutterstock.com, p121
Dmitry Sheremeta/Shutterstock.com,
p136-137
donatas1205/Shutterstock, p51, 53, 55, 76
Dudarev Mikhail/Shutterstock.com, p18-19
Elina Manninen/Shutterstock.com, p101
Erik Mandre/Shutterstock.com, p96-97
Falcona/shutterstock.com, p54
FCSCAFEINE/Shutterstock.com, p87
Fesus Robert/Shutterstock.com, p152
Flas100/Shutterstock.com, p64, 65, 88-89,
92-93, 128-129, 156-157
frankie's/Shutterstock.com, p154-155
gillmar/Shutterstock.com, p71
Igor Zh/Shutterstock.com, p38-39
Jacob Lund/Shutterstock.com, p26-27
Jule_Berlin/Shutterstock.com, p84
KellyNelson/Shutterstock.com, p106-107
khan3145/Shutterstock.com, p22-23
kukuruxa/Shutterstock.com, p120
Le Panda/Shutterstock.com, p17, 122-123,
145
Leonid Ikan/Shutterstock.com, p46-47
Lily Sab/Shutterstock.com, p34-35
Little Perfect Stock/Shutterstock.com, p113
Magnia/Shutterstock.com, p45, 78
Maria Savenko/Shutterstock.com, p94-95
mika_kika/Shutterstock.com p3, 33, 61, 81,
96-97, 112, 127, 135
Monika Gniot/Shutterstock.com, p114
mrmohock/Shutterstock.com, p102-103

mythja/Shutterstock.com, p58, 148
Natali Zakharova/Shutterstock.com, p12, 56
Naviya/Shutterstock.com, p119
Neale Cousland/Shutterstock.com, p133
OHoHO/Shutterstock.com, p74-p75
oriontrail/Shutterstock.com, p146-147
Ozerov Alexander/Shutterstock.com, p8
photolinc/Shutterstock.com, p85
Pics-xl/Shutterstock.com, p80
pixelheadphoto digitalskillet/Shutterstock.
com, p111
PopTika/Shutterstock.com, p57
Prostock-studio/Shutterstock.com, p29
Rawpixel.com/Shutterstock.com, p132
Rich Carey/Shutterstock.com, p69
Room 76/Shutterstock.com, p122-123
sanao/Shutterstock.com, p90-91
Sanja Karin Music/Shutterstock.com,
p124-125
SantiPhotoSS/Shutterstock.com, p151
sNike/Shutterstock.com, p14-15
solarbird/Shutterstock.com, p16, 72, 115, 150
solarseven/Shutterstock.com, p144
Stone36/Shutterstock.com, p66-67
Subbotina Anna/Shutterstock.com, p110,
130-131
SueC/Shutterstock.com, p108-109
sumire8/Shutterstock.com, p59
Sundari/Shutterstock.com, p40-41
Syrytsyna Tetiana/Shutterstock, p4, 48,
64-65
tgergo/Shutterstock.com, p139
Tina Bits/Shutterstock.com, p138
UliAb/Shutterstock.com, p142
vector illustration/Shutterstock.com, p59,
62-63, 68, 69, 73, 74-75, 76, 78, 98-99, 104,
110, 111, 116-117, 119, 121, 122-123, 126, 149
Vishnevskiy Vasily/Shutterstock.com,
p92-93
windmoon/Shutterstock.com, p82-83
zhangyang13576997233/Shutterstock.com,
p62-63

*Backgrounds used throughout:*
Ratana21/Shutterstock.com
one AND only/Shutterstock.com
Berezina/Shutterstock.com

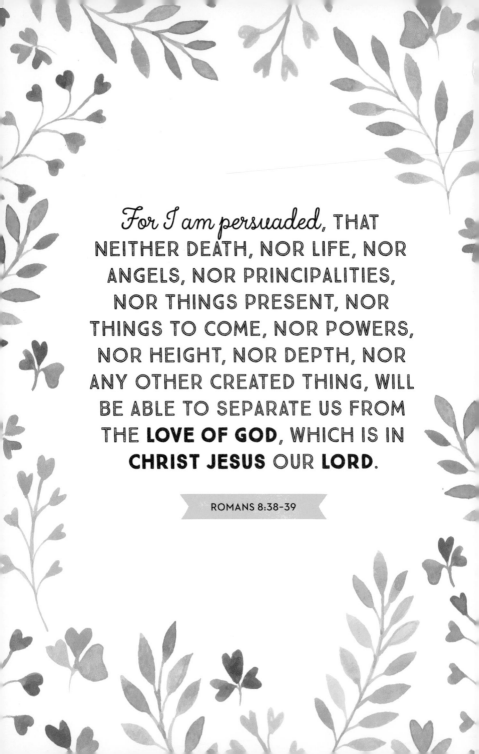

For I am persuaded, THAT NEITHER DEATH, NOR LIFE, NOR ANGELS, NOR PRINCIPALITIES, NOR THINGS PRESENT, NOR THINGS TO COME, NOR POWERS, NOR HEIGHT, NOR DEPTH, NOR ANY OTHER CREATED THING, WILL BE ABLE TO SEPARATE US FROM THE **LOVE OF GOD**, WHICH IS IN **CHRIST JESUS** OUR **LORD**.

ROMANS 8:38–39